FAMILY RESEMBLANCES

MARY BURRITT CHRISTIANSEN POETRY SERIES

Hilda Raz, *Series Editor*

Mary Burritt
Christiansen
Poetry Series

The Mary Burritt Christiansen Poetry Series publishes
two to four books a year that engage and give voice to the
realities of living, working, and experiencing the West and
the Border as places and as metaphors. The purpose of the
series is to expand access to, and the audience for, quality
poetry, both single volumes and anthologies, that can be
used for general reading as well as in classrooms.

Also available in the Mary Burritt Christiansen Poetry Series:

The Woman Who Married a Bear: Poems by Tiffany Midge
Self-Portrait with Spurs and Sulfur: Poems by Casey Thayer
Crossing Over: Poems by Priscilla Long
Heresies: Poems by Orlando Ricardo Menes
Report to the Department of the Interior: Poems by Diane Glancy
The Sky Is Shooting Blue Arrows: Poems by Glenna Luschei
A Selected History of Her Heart: Poems by Carole Simmons Oles
The Arranged Marriage: Poems by Jehanne Dubrow
The Goldilocks Zone by Kate Gale
Flirt by Noah Blaustein

For additional titles in the Mary Burritt Christiansen Poetry Series, please
visit unmpress.com.

FAMILY RESEMBLANCES

poems

Carrie Shipers

University of New Mexico Press | Albuquerque

Printed in the United States of America
21 20 19 18 17 16   1 2 3 4 5 6

Library of Congress Cataloging-in-Publication Data
Shipers, Carrie.
  [Poems. Selections]
  Family resemblances : poems / Carrie Shipers.
      pages cm. — (Mary Burritt Christiansen Poetry Series)
  ISBN 978-0-8263-5654-3 (pbk. : alk. paper) — ISBN 978-0-8263-5655-0 (electronic)
  I. Title.
  PS3619.H5776A6 2016
  811'.6—dc23

                              2015018219

Cover illustration courtesy of Pixabay
Author photo by Kyah Jo Stangl
Designed by Felicia Cedillos
Composed in Dante 10.5/15

For my parents, who let me steal their stories.

Contents

One

Two

Three

ONE

Rescue Conditions

Like fairy tales, my mother's stories were meant
to order the world: *Once, there was a fourteen-*
year-old girl, a windshield, a barbed wire fence.
Once, there was a man your father knew,
a gravel road, a cargo rack, a passenger
pinned like a frog. I used to imagine myself
victim of more benign emergencies:
a fainting spell at school; a car accident
with no injuries except one long, dramatic cut
that wouldn't scar; my head hitting the gym floor
so hard no one would let me move. I wanted
to be rescued from what wasn't my fault,
the stretcher and straps a glass coffin to bear away
my blameless body. Instead, I was bitten
by a poisonous spider. I broke my ankle,
caught bronchitis, was dehydrated by the flu.
I lived by the rules my mother made:
Wear your seat belt. Stay away from guns.
Don't drink or take rides from people who do.
Lie to me and you'll be sorry. Always,
I heard warnings she wouldn't say: *If you die*
in pieces on a dirt road it takes two hours to find;
if you slit your lover's throat and try to slit
your own, trailing blood all over the house;
if you fall down in a cornfield and no one knows
till you start to rot—don't make me be who finds you.
I never said how much I needed to be found,
to feel her gloved hands holding mine and know
she'd save me even from the ending I deserved.

November, 1964

His father says a man needs land
of his own, but his uncles
want him to go to college first.
They're crazy, all of them, always
turning up broke and hungry,
wearing baggy prison suits.
Himself, he's not too sure
how much of the world he wants
to see. He learned in school
that the stars don't stand still,
but when he cruises the river bottoms
in his yellow Mercury, he feels
as though they do. Sundays
after church there's chores
and a fried-chicken dinner,
and when the men go to the porch
to drink iced tea, he doesn't have
a lot to say, and isn't expected to.

Treatment Plan

In April 2008, Suzy Bass, a popular high school math teacher in Knoxville, TN, was revealed to be faking her diagnosis of stage IV breast cancer. Unlike many people who fake cancer, she did not benefit from her lies financially.

When I was sick, I didn't have to be my best self
every second, could forget friends' birthdays,
why they wouldn't eat meat. People loved me
without hair, with radiation tattoos I drew
with permanent marker, rashes from a rolled-up towel
rubbed hard against my skin. The more I asked,
the more they gave—cleaned my house, covered
my classes, drove an hour for pomegranates
or pumpkin soup. Not everything I did was bad.
I raised awareness, money for research, showed
how hard survival is. I inspired walkathons
and silent auctions, people's refusal to give up
on a cure, on me, even when I smelled like sweat
and vomit. If I hadn't gotten caught I would've had
to fake remission, watch friends forget how sick
I'd been. The doctors here don't ask me how I feel.
Lonely, I'd say if they did. Afraid to live without
the sickness I invented, sympathy that made me real.

Renovation

For emily and Erica

The pickaxe he bought for my birthday,
pitchfork when he proposed. A power saw
at Christmas. On our first anniversary—

Sheetrock, nail gun, boxes of tile. All the time
he was dying I held his love in my hands,
unrolled plans across his lap. His X rays

read like blueprints—here a tumor, here
a fireplace, bay window seat, sickness
surgeons couldn't reach. I brought him home

to watch me build, muffled my hammer,
worked mostly when the morphine did.
After he died, I sleepwalked, woke holding

tools to cut or burn or dig. I tore up beds
of tulips, taped an X on antique glass and tapped
its center. My grief cut wires, twisted pipes,

set fires I barely found in time. Awake,
I built our home. Asleep, his monument.

Vocational Training

I sound so much like my mother
that when people called our house for help,
I'd have to stop them halfway through
their stories. *Hold on*, I'd say, *I'm not her.*
When I went with her on calls, I hovered
in doorways, holding her equipment, watched
her walk to the center of what was wrong.
I knew I could memorize facts, anatomy,
the math of giving oxygen or shock,
but I needed her to teach me what the body
wanted. What I learned was common sense:
*Apply pressure to bleeding. Stay as calm
as you can.* I'll never have her hands,
the power I saw her wield, but sometimes
I feel her voice in my mouth: *Get some ice
and you'll be fine. It doesn't need stitches,
it's only a scratch.* Even when I'm the one
speaking, my mother's voice knows what to do.

Kitchen Wars

She trusts bare feet between his steel-toed boots,
the hem of her blouse to his fist when they kiss
good-bye, then snaps her dish towel hard.
By the time the stove gives out, she'll have stripped
its enamel with scrubbing, all the mornings
like this one, children still in bed, or the nights
she waits as long as she can to feed them again,
then waits for his truck in the drive. How long
it takes him to kill the engine and open his door
tells her where he's been, whether he'll want
the plate she's saved and bread to wipe it clean,
want her to wait for morning before she washes
one more dish. Even if he doesn't eat,
she stays, watching what he doesn't want seen,
how slowly he takes off his boots, fingers thick
around a bottle or can, voice thick with tears
he can only cry if she does first. She isn't what
or who he wants to hurt, but his anger
moves fast as a fist. In the kitchen she knows
where everything is: knives sliding in their drawer,
cast-iron skillet tucked in the oven, glass
measuring cup on the highest shelf beside
her three good plates and deviled-egg platter,
each hollow curved like a shell in reverse. She knows
she has to win against what hurts them both.

Appetite

In the forest, my brother ate bread crumbs, berries,
half the witch's house before she captured us.
The walk home took two weeks. His greasy thighs
broke out in rashes, chins wobbled when he cried,

gobbled the gingerbread I'd packed for our trip.
Our second stepmother was kinder than our first,
brought us bread and mugs of milk. When I talked
about the witch I said, *We got away*, swallowed

the oven's cast-iron clang, her breathy screams.
Game was scarce but there was enough
if we were careful. One morning before dawn
our stepmother led me to the larder: *He's eaten half*

of what we have. In another month we'll starve.
I sent her to the forest to help my father, fed Hansel
his breakfast outside. After he ate he fell asleep,
his head tipped back, plump throat exposed.

My fingers found the knife. In the kitchen,
I rubbed a tender flank with salt, butter, sage,
opened the oven door. I'll say he ran away,
that he missed the witch's sweets and stories,

and while I talk I'll dish up supper—black pudding,
potatoes, a roast as sweet as suckling pig.

Elizabeth King Explains Why *Pupil,*
Her One-Half Life-Size Sculpture, Is a Self-Portrait

To be myself with more precision
than flesh and blood allow. To outlive
my skin, inspire damage I know

I can repair. To admire my lovely arms.
To disarm unease, deconstruct dismay.
To animate unknowing and know

I am well made. To scale ambition,
enlarge encounter, astonish
and distill. To access artifice, arrest

perception, enrich my intent. To make
my offices less lonely and austere.
To see myself the size I really am.

Whereabouts, Last Known

My sister disappeared two months ago. She owes
back rent, cable and electric bills. I haven't seen
her photograph—Missing, Possibly at Risk—
on the news, taped to telephone poles or plate glass.
No one's called to question me, suggest a search.
If I drove ninety minutes, begged the landlord
to let me in, would I find an address book
or a calendar, each scribbled square a clue?
Does she have a computer, saved e-mails
and archived chats, list of websites labeled
"History"? I don't know if she carries a purse,
cell phone, pepper spray. If her body's found
in a cornfield or abandoned house,
I couldn't name a single friend, lover, suspect.

If I went to the police, they'd ask when I last saw
or spoke to her. Six months ago I rushed her
off the phone, bored by her hello. *Has she been
missing before?* Two, eight, and thirteen years ago.
*Does she have debts or sketchy friends, a man
she might be with?* Yes, probably, I don't know.
In a TV movie I'd search on my own, open a tip line,
offer a reward. I'd hand out fliers on weekends,
evenings after work. I wouldn't think my sister
disappeared on purpose, that eventually she'll call
and act like nothing happened, that when she does,
I'll be more impatient than relieved.

Shelbina Jailbreak

He's sleeping it off in a corner cell
when three guys from Texarkana ask
if he wants out. He can tell by the way
they talk they're in for something worse
than a bar fight or stolen car, so he points
to his blood-stiffened shirt—on payday
Saturday nights he and the rest
of the Ma Bell boys throw fists
like shaking hands—and tells them *no*,
not mentioning his unlocked cell
or the tin cups of coffee the jailer brings
at dawn. He lies on his cot and counts
to a hundred, thinking of corncrib
hide-and-seek with his brothers, then opens
his cell and calls the sheriff, who shakes
his hand and has a deputy drop him off
at the phone-company barracks.

Sunday shifts pay double and he works
every one, sends money home
to his girl—they're saving for a house—
and drinks what's left. Until August,
when all the work is done, he spends
each day digging holes and laying phone lines
and filling the holes back up again,
wondering if he should've said *yes*,
if it's better to be worn out by freedom,
like the men he meets who make
the rounds of county lockups, or to be
like his father, worn down by work.

In December, he'll borrow fifty dollars and a suit
to testify at the trial. He'll be married
by then, almost a father, and when he takes
the stand he'll know for sure:
men like him aren't meant for escape.

Memoriam: Flight

Fish from Woolworth's died right away, turtles
    disappeared, white mice ate their babies, slept
        until she let them go. Canaries lost their feathers,

spilled seed on the basement floor. She'd coo
    and whistle to make them sing, but they danced
        to Lou's accordion, pink feet shuffling

on Saturday mornings. Just off the night shift
    at Continental Can, he played polka till the neighbors
        called: *Would you open the windows, please,*

so everyone can hear? Even more than keeping
    canaries she loved to let them go, the first flutter
        of wings almost a shiver, the world of grass

and sun a wondrous thing—later she'd realize
    they were raised in cages—then they were gone.
        Lou said nothing pretty went to waste, brought home

hair ribbons, flowers from neighbors' yards.
    Walking to his grave she watches the ground
        for pale flashes of fur, trees for golden heads

and feathers, canaries flocking over Omaha, perched
    on rooftops and power lines on Hillsdale Avenue,
        nesting on headstones in Graceland Park,

marking every place she'd been his daughter.

Driving Lessons

It was my father's fault I drove too fast
on the snaking blacktop he took to work.
Sixty-five and no brakes, he'd say,
and later I'd report, *Sixty-eight*—
but I never crashed the red Beretta
I bought instead of his first choice,
something safe and square I'd need
two hands to turn. My second year
of college, spring break ended in a blizzard.
Before he'd let me leave, he tested me
on unplowed streets. *Only hold on
as hard as you have to. Know how fast
you can go.* At an icy intersection
five years later, I braked too hard
and started to skid, then cut my wheels
and tapped the brake. Six inches
before the line, the car stopped straight
in its lane. I imagined my father
beside me, hands braced on the dash,
face cracking open in a grin. When he taught me
what I'd need to know to leave him,
I think he knew how much of him I'd keep.

Autopsy

Dr. David Bassett spent 17 years dissecting human cadavers to create the
25-volume Stereoscopic Atlas of Human Anatomy. He died at age 52 from a
combination of rare diseases that caused his internal organs to thicken.

My scalpel draws skin away from secrets,
slices through fascia that holds our parts
in place. In med school, panicked, sleepless,

I saw through strangers' skin, bone and sinew
belonging to a man in a diner, woman in the park.
My wife's sweet jaw. Our baby's fingers.

Formaldehyde hardens organs, turns tissue
gray. I invented a fixative that preserves
but doesn't distort, dyes that follow

every branch of artery and vein, maps I need
to make my atlas. I saved for last the hand,
neck, skull, what makes us most ourselves.

Every hour I parse nerve and muscle,
chemicals meant to keep the dead
leach into living tissue, my lungs and brain.

If I opened my chest, reached inside,
would I find my organs thickening, colors
bright but dull, the work of my body

stopped one cell at a time? I've written
instructions, cut by cut, diagrammed
what I believe will cause my death.

Medical History

I wanted it: arc of red and blue
strobing my skin, sirens singing
my praises, the cinching embrace
of the cot as the ambulance
slammed shut and steered away.
More than needle-pierce
or dragging blade, I wanted the swab
of alcohol and cotton, the promise
of gauze-covered cure.
My mother saved anyone
who asked, but never me,
never the way I wanted:
her palms skimming my limbs
for injury, her fingers finding
what hurt, her lips whispering,
I got here just in time.

Kill Switch

Each time he fit my hand to something new
he taught me what to guard against, how to keep
from slicing the cord, the switch or button

to hit if I got scared. In the woods, he warned:
If you start to fall, throw the saw as hard
as you can. In the shop: *Watch your fingers.*

We can buy more boards. I loved the shriek
of saw and drill, vibrations shaking my arms,
wood chips hitting my shoes. I learned to weld,

to clamp and strike, sew metal seams. If I lost
my nerve, stopped blade or motor midway—
gears jam, belts whip themselves broken,

teeth bite what they can reach—he knew
he'd taught me well. My greatest fear:
the machine of his body breaking, kill switch

tripping inside his brain. In the silence that follows
the final cut, you can hear the sawdust fall.

The Woman Who Can't Forget: Self-Storage

Jill Price was the first person to be diagnosed with what scientists have termed hyperthymestic syndrome. Her autobiographical memory is so strong that she remembers virtually every event in her life from the age of fourteen.

My first matryoshka: blonde peasant girls
with braids, red pinafores, pink blushing cheeks,
each opening to reveal a smaller, identical self,

the last no larger than my thumb. I like best
the ones that change: Yeltsin, Gorbachev, Stalin;
elephant, tiger, bear. Inside me, every self

I've ever been: the girl who thought her mom
would die if she gained weight, left for college
with cardboard boxes she carried home

midterm. The woman who lied to her husband,
got fired for correcting her boss. Matryoshkas
crowd my mantel, bookcase, shelves—I can't stand

to leave them stacked. My old selves breathe,
shudder, speak, each convinced it knows me
best, knows better than I do now. Mornings,

I recite their names, how and when I got them,
make sure each set's complete. If any one
went missing, it would leave a hollow space.

Portrait

Cheekbones blessed with freckles
and light, he smiles at the camera
or my mother behind it. Red hair
curls past the collar of his Western-
style shirt. The hand I can see
is holding a beer, the other—
maybe the straw Stetson last seen
two decades later, keys to a car
he rides into cornfields and ditches.
All my life I've tried to understand
the parts of him I was born too late
to see. If I stepped into the frame,
startled him by being the child
he doesn't plan to have, I'm not sure
what I hope he'd say. I know more
about his future than he'd ever ask.

Father and Son

After Anne Sexton

You turned eighteen steering west—
one hand on the wheel,
the other clenched. Question me
the fights we had—tools
left in the rain, grass killed
by careless oil. Answer me
my bloody nose, your broken
knuckles. Question me.
I'd take it all back if I could.

Long distance, I warn:
The desert makes a man
awful dry. You crack a beer:
I'm not like you. Question me
about this and I'll open my hood,
hand you my finest ratchet.
Answer me your sparest part,
your shiny spark plug,
thrown piston and rebuilt block.

In my dreams you race a red sun
across the Arizona sky,
your tailpipe spewing sand.
Every day I watch the weather
for Phoenix, wanting you to burn
white-hot and head for home.

Field Guide

She married him for what he knew—
names of trees, animals, how to hot-wire
his Mercury when he lost his keys. Beside him
on the wide bench seat, she'd point to birds
standing in the road, flying overhead:
*crested sparrow, blue-banded snipe, brown-
tailed hawk.* They had three kids before
she caught on. *What bird is that?* she asked
as they sat on the porch, babies asleep upstairs.
Jewel-bellied swallow, he said, *you can tell
by the beak,* and just like that she knew. *Tell me,*
she said. His mouth twitched. *I don't know.*
Later, she wondered as she handed him tools:
Did he make up *socket wrench? Phillips head?*

*We won't go hungry. That cut looks worse
than it is.* For years, she lied by pretending
to know what she only hoped, each time hoping
he'd catch her out so she could tell the truth:
I'm scared, too. Children grown, too late
to confess, she stands at the kitchen sink,
wondering if he'd believed her lies or lied
by seeming to. *What bird is that?* she asks.
He calls from another room, *Three-toed warbler.*

Inheritance

After a line by Bob Hicok

I want your wink, your luck at cards, grip
on the cue when the eight ball sinks, stories

you tell so well I believe you every time.
You redheaded stepchild, I want your curls,

your curses, the *Damn me* and *Go to hell*
you never mean. I want your drive,

the blacktop swerve and almost-hit, tickets
you talked your way out of. Your fix,

your wrenching, take-it-apart-and-try-again.
I want your build, sawdust sweat and hammer

swing. Your level, your know-what's-plumb.
I want your fists, your fury, door slam

instead of shudder. Your tender, your teach.
Your weather eye, your wait and see.

Landing Gear

For a week, I fall down stairs. The first time
is also the worst. I think, *I'm going to fall,*
then do, a full flight outside a basement classroom.
On the way down, I coach myself to arch
my back, tuck chin to chest, curve my arm
around my unzipped bag. Afterward, I sit
on the bottom step till I'm sure I won't cry.
Within days, I misjudge two concrete steps outside
my apartment and fall to my knees, tearing pants
and palm. A dark half flight near my office,
a broken nail. A second half flight Friday.

My mother blames high heels, no breakfast,
a tendency to do one thing and think of another.
I consider the hospital, where doctors will test
my reflexes, scan my brain, disbelieve my story.
In college, neck aching from the weight
of my waitressing apron, I saw a doctor
who asked, *Is someone hurting you?*
He gave me pamphlets, a prescription
I didn't fill. Later, I tried to be grateful he'd asked,
just as I tried to be the time my mother,
after weeks of unhappy phone calls from Ohio,
said, *He doesn't hit you, does he?*

I watch my bruises fade and change their shape,
interpreting them the way I knew I would—
as evidence of bravery, a hardy disregard
for pain. I begin to craft the story, *the week
I fell down stairs,* as though it belongs
to someone else. Always, the story ends
with laughter at my lack of grace
and serious injury instead of what was really
after: my swollen ankle zipped inside my boot,
hand gripping, not skimming, the railing,
how hard I had to think on my way down.

TWO

Story Problem

The Alaska pipeline runs through St. Louis,
my father says. Every two weeks,
twenty-five miles of fifty-foot trench.
Sixty-two dollars an hour. Ten years
since I left home. I call him every week,
greedy for stories: the pterodactyl
that attacked his truck; weather so hot
or cold concrete won't set; the oatmeal
his grandmother served to cure
his teenage drinking. *They're moving
pretty fast*, he says. *I'd have to join up soon.*
At fifty-nine, he's awake by four-thirty.
When he visits, he sleeps sitting up, leaves
before breakfast even though I buy biscuits,
bacon, powdered gravy to stir into milk.
They're a rough-looking bunch, he says.
I know he won't really go. He says
stories aren't lies if you tell them right.

Moose Liquor

Even at eighteen, he didn't push
his luck buying 3.2 beer across
the Kansas line. He only filled the trunk,
not the Mercury's big backseat,
with cases he carried four at a time.
His last trip, he was two bucks short
but the owner waved away
his offer to unload: *You're good
for it, son. I know you'll be back.*

He was speeding home to Missouri
when he heard the siren. In Kansas,
he was old enough to drink the beer
he bought, but crossing state lines
was a crime. The trooper wrote out
a ten-dollar ticket. *Looks to me
your back end's riding low,* he said.
You better check your shocks.

To see himself as an outlaw,
he has to forget how the story ends:
not with a police chase or time
served, but his sheepish smile,
his careful drive away from a debt—
two dollars and luck—he never paid.

The Woman Who Can't Forget: Friendship

It's lonely to remember so much: the eighth-grade
spelling bee I lost on *deficiency*, one-night stand
I thought I loved, every time you've rushed me

off the phone, forgotten our plans. You remember
the afternoon you helped me find the perfect dress,
sweater, bathing suit—you aren't sure which,

the time you left work early because I needed you.
You hated that job, asked me to call the Wednesday
your report was due. I told the receptionist

my mom was sick and I was scared. Four years later,
my lie came true. I'll never forget the salad
you had for lunch three years ago last Thursday,

your lover's home address, lipstick I watched
you steal, what you said in our last fight, when
your husband proposed. You need someone

to keep your secrets, keep track of every stupid,
shameful thing you've done and love you
anyway. For you I'll be the friend I'll never have.

Trust Jesus:

                     block letters painted
under every overpass I knew, words

I looked for as I drove toward curfew,
turning off the interstate to test myself

on curving blacktops. Even when I passed
I had to pull over—eyes closed,

hands clenching the wheel, grateful
I hadn't been caught, arrested, killed.

If the painter had appeared to me then,
index finger stained blue or stinging

with gasoline, would I have seen
what we shared? Afraid every headlight

was the highway patrol, each night
driving farther to find blank space,

my crime, like his, an act of faith.

Marriage

Talk of war upsets him more than you'd think
for a man who didn't go. Most nights he does
his fighting at home, marching dead soldiers
across the kitchen table while she feeds the kids.
He knows he's mean when he drinks—
he's glad he gave away his guns—
but explaining *why* comes out like her fault
and he storms out the screen door to his truck.

When he comes home he'll use his pocketknife
to peel enough potatoes for the two of them,
enough for the kids, the neighbors, too. By the time
he lights the stove, he'll know she isn't hungry.
She won't get up when he burns his hand,
cursing just loud enough not to wake the baby,
or when he scrapes fried potatoes onto a plate
and scrambles three eggs, not even when he slams
the breadbox door and holds his breath, waiting.

In the morning he'll be long gone for work
before she finds the mess he's left—
stovetop clotted with grease, eggshells burnt
to the bottom of her best skillet, two pounds
of potatoes turning black in the sink. He'll come home
hungry for a fight, smash a dozen empty bottles
on the back step, but she won't even blink,
just hand him the broom and go back to washing dishes.
The cleaning up is worse than the breaking,
he'll want to say, but forgets as soon as he can.

Job Description

He thinks my work will bring bad luck,
disease or sorrow I can't shake. *Tending*
strangers by the side of the road, he says,
you'll get yourself hurt. I've tried
to prove how safe I am, the gloves
and sterile pads, radio clipped to my belt,
my partner always close by. He doesn't see
how much I need disasters that aren't mine,
to know I can fix what isn't my fault.
Our first ten years were one emergency
after the other, him or the kids or me,
always someone bleeding, fevered, scared,
and all I could offer was peroxide
and aspirin, reasons why we'd be okay.
In my uniform, I walk into someone else's mess
of unwashed dishes or broken glass, pry open
car doors crushed against their frames.
With my flashlight, I shed what light I can.

Lost, Damaged, Delayed

The first time, I only borrowed, left a catalog
in my truck—organic sheets, handwoven rugs—
delivered it next day. Then a magazine packed

with lip gloss and scarves. Two weeks later
I bought a replacement I kicked down stairs,
dipped in the sink, delivered in a plastic bag

printed with apologies. I never took anything
Priority or *Express*, that looked like a check
or bill. Still, there were too many choices:

Occupant, Safe Driver, Generous Friend;
greeting cards in colored envelopes; catalogs
for clothes, bicycle parts, vacation homes;

letters stacked in every drawer and closet,
the kitchen sink, till my route had the most
lost mail in Michigan. When people say

they feel betrayed, exposed, their secrets
torn open and tossed aside, I want to explain
how tenderly I read letters they shouldn't see,

junk mail they wouldn't want, how hard I cried
once my house was empty—all those words
I'll never read, envelopes sealed against me.

The Dollmaker's Daughter

Headless bodies, necks slip-stitched like sacks,
filled her workroom. I gave them names
and stories, rocked them to sleep, dressed them

for school or walks outside. Mama hated heads
that looked like dolls instead of people—yarn-
haired plastic, porcelain with matching hands—

learned to cast and mold her own. The first ones
had my face. Then she learned our mailman's
crooked lips and shell-shaped ears. Mama loves

her dolls until the final stitch. She'll never miss
the ones I've sold. I need money for the road,
a motel like the one we stayed in once. When she

took a shower, I saw that nothing in our room—
not the flowers on the curtains, the rocks and water
framed above our beds—had eyes to see

what I might do. She tells me I'm her first,
best doll. She doesn't know what's in my head.

Mechanical Failure

What cars could make men do: bleed, curse,
throw wrenches. Grin, swagger, clap

each other's backs. Women worried
about money, what to fix for meals, what might

be broken and how they'd know. Men broke,
then fixed with hands like my father's, brother's—

grease ground under the skin, fingernails flat
and square. I wanted their hands, wanted to say

piston, crankshaft, manifold, and mean it like a man,
wash to the elbow with Lava, GOJO, forget

to rinse the sink, be reckless with paper towels.
I failed at work that didn't choose me, hands

stuttering wrenches, throat swallowing names
of parts. I quit the shop, quit thinking

the only power was what men knew, machines
and how to tend them. Their work was easier

than women's: understanding men, tending
their hurts, knuckles and hearts scraped raw

by a mysterious, clumsy force, themselves.

House Rules

I.

Saturday nights he circles the table—
clack of balls and buzzing juke—
swigs from cool brown bottles, wipes
hands on jeans and reaches
for the chalk. When someone suggests
a bet, he pretends he isn't sure, gives in
when his opponent offers him the break.
He's working an extra shift—pool cue
instead of a hammer—and he only loses
when he needs to. The old men
playing snooker know what he's doing
but don't give him up, laying down
their cues to watch a whole night's
worth of luck settle in his shoulders.

2.

It's true he hustles when he has to—
three kids, then four, wife stretching his pay
so far they snap at each other in their sleep,
him drinking less than he wants but still
too much—but he can't stand how it
becomes a habit, how he's always working
angles that aren't on the table. One night
in a roadhouse two towns over he bends
to line up his shot—fingers so slick with sweat
he almost drops his granddad's cue—
and isn't sure if he's trying to win or lose.

Craftsmanship

My mother can't make sense of this:
duct tape cut, not torn, the precise angles

of PVC from exhaust pipe to truck window,
a man she'd known for years inhaling poison

while his wife waited at home. He'd never
stayed gone longer than a day, missed work

without calling, qualities my mother admires
that make his death even harder to understand.

In the photographs she saw—chin pressed
to chest, thermos and jacket on the seat—

he could be sleeping after too much beer or work.
She understands accidents, bad luck leading

to disaster, but not surrender, the decision
not to survive. Before he started the engine,

he put away his tools—knife, tape, hacksaw
used to cut the pipe—and closed the toolbox lid.

Olympia

After E. T. A. Hoffmann

Her skin feels just like flesh, bruises if I hold
her arms too tight, bleeds when she tears her lip.
In Japan, a caller reported a woman's body

wrapped in a blanket. In the morgue, the coroner
discovered the woman was a life-size doll.
I wonder how he could tell, if he made the first cut,

then another, discovered gears or empty space
instead of organs. In the lab I work on joints—
ball socket, pivot, hinge—for robots that don't

have faces, just circuit boards and motion sensors.
After she moved in, I saw how cold she was,
how when I yelled she made her face go blank.

She sleeps against the wall, legs curved
away from me. I didn't know machines
could breathe, bite their nails and need to shower,

be programmed to flinch, cry, hide in closets,
under our bed. If she were real she wouldn't
let me smash her phone, control her food.

The lab has everything I need—saws, clamps,
long-nose pliers, a camera to record my work.
I'll disconnect her power before the cutting starts.

White Lung

When he left the farm in '48 he wanted
steady work and a garden big enough
for corn, tomatoes, squash. Thirty years
of factory work, close air reeking of sweat
and dye, lint clotting narrow lungs. *Unroll,
measure, cut.* Left hand unfurled the bolt,
right hand scissored, grew hard and yellow
at the joints. *Unroll, measure, cut.*
He knew the cough was coming, felt it prick
and sting his chest. *Bronchitis, strep throat,
pneumonia.* He tried to tell his wife.

He longs for something sweet—watermelon,
maybe, or peaches. She offers applesauce
in a plastic-coated spoon. In the garden,
a fist-size cantaloupe too green to smell.
You'll never keep it down. She wipes
his face and chest with a dishrag gone sour.
In the morning she sweeps around his sickbed.
In the afternoon she hangs out wash.

Organe Failure

A man who received a heart transplant 12 years ago and later married the donor's widow died the same way the donor did, authorities said: of a self-inflicted gunshot wound.

—"Man kills self 12 years after receiving heart from suicide victim,"
ASSOCIATED PRESS, APRIL 6, 2008

Sonny signed his letter, *With all my borrowed*
heart. The week before, he tried to warn me.
When I die, he said. I laid my hand on his chest.
It won't be soon. Straight through his throat,
no bone to deflect the bullet. Terry and I
were high school sweethearts, but we didn't
stay sweet. One day he took his rifle
into the woods, his aim off just enough to leave
him breathing, brain-dead. Even as a kid
he thought too much, kept what he felt inside.
Sonny shared everything he had—bought
a washer and dryer for a family with six kids,
found jobs for folks who needed them.
When I couldn't pay my rent, he bought a house,
put the title in my name. I worried what people
would say—him thirty years older and rich
besides—but Sonny knew I loved him.

We were married eleven years. Reporters
crowded his funeral, some I'd seen at the wedding.
They asked if Terry's heart was cursed. Tell me,
how do you answer a question like that? *No,*
the heart's an ugly fist of muscle that doesn't feel
a thing. *Yes,* if it's not the heart, it must be me.

The Worst

I played a patient at demonstrations
and training classes because I was easy
to lift. Once, as I slumped in the front seat
of a pickup, my mother screamed, *My baby,
I have to see my baby.* The medic being tested
put his body between us. She pushed him
hard against the arm I claimed was broken.
As she totaled his score, she said, *If she
were really my daughter, I would have gone
right through you.* When my mother imagined
the worst, she knew what she feared—
not the phone call after dark, patrolman
knocking at her door, but gravel embedded
in my scalp, brain leaking onto my shoulder,
the body shaped like hers twisted into what
she didn't know. Her reward for witnessing
the worst so many mothers feared: to imagine,
always, her daughter's face in place of theirs.

Waiting for Spring

Mud sucks the boots off his feet and the hot
from his coffee till his hammer goes clumsy
with cold. All fall he drives home dripping.
It could be worse, he tells his wife, stripping
his muddy jeans on newspapers spread
by the kitchen door. *At least I'm working.*
After the factory killed his father, he swore
he'd work outside. He hadn't been thinking
of snow, gray afternoons spent hauling brush
or shoveling scrap wood at the mill for cash
creased into his pocket. If he stops
in a bar he goes home guilty—four kids
he can barely keep in milk. There's no overtime
for unemployment even though he earns it
in his dreams, breathing sawdust and sweat
while his family sleeps. He wakes up wanting
whiskey but settles for a beer, pretending
he can't hear his father say with every swallow:
Men who drink their pride are always thirsty.

The Woman Who Can't Forget: Flooding

*In Greek mythology, the river Mnemosyne, named for the goddess of memory, runs
through Hades and is the counterpart to Lethe, the river of forgetting.*

Rain, rising water, sirens crying *disaster.*
Sandbags, shovels, everything you love

on the highest shelf. Instinct says *swim,*
but you can hardly tread water. No rescue boats,

helicopters; no one to throw a rope, hold out
a branch. Amid floating trash, debris

you recognize: yearbooks, toys you had
or wanted, wedding gown. Your head

goes under once, twice. When the flood
recedes, you spit brown water, grit,

something sour like regret. While you
were underwater, the landscape changed.

People look at you strangely, wonder why
your clothes are wet, why you track sand

with every step. You smell of mud and rotting
fish, memories meant to stay submerged.

Safe Return

On the news, we thanked the FBI,
local and state police, volunteers, everyone
who helped us bring our daughter home.
We asked for privacy while she recovered

but were sure she wouldn't need counseling,
just a night-light, new clothes, patience
when she acted out. She came home
with bloody socks and no underwear.

She has lice and open sores, wrecks the toys
we bought every birthday, Christmas
she was gone. At night we lock her door
so she won't hurt the baby, look for the gun

she thinks we have. If we say *no* she bites,
goes for our eyes with pencils and plastic
knives. Every day we pray, try to remember
she's just a child, a little girl who survived

a terrible ordeal. She's a brat, an animal,
an eight-year-old demon we don't deserve.
Our nightmare isn't over. What they found
isn't yet—might never be—our daughter.

Witness

She says, *I never knew how much you heard.*
Everything, I think, *not nearly enough.*
Even more than her bloody uniform, bruises
under her eyes, my mother brought home stories.
I say, *Enough to know what bothered you.*
She sighs. *There wasn't much. I used to wonder*
what I'd become, if everything I saw
came off with the uniform. Mornings
she came home quiet and rocked in her chair,
coffee going cold in her hand, I knew
she had a story. At first, she tried to save them
for friends at work or for my father, who'd whisper
Jesus Christ and push away his plate.

There were some things, she says. *The babies,*
or that woman they found. She doesn't know
how hard I listened, worried she'd stop
if she remembered who I was. Before she goes,
I try to say something wise, something she
might say to me—practical, but not unkind.
Mom, I say, *if you felt bad all the time,*
you wouldn't have been much help. She says,
Maybe, then *Good-bye*, and I'm afraid
I haven't heard the story she needs to tell.

THREE

War Stories

Days, in the factory that killed his father,
he blocked caps with crooked fingers, knuckles
smashed flat or ridged from being broken.
Nights, he drank and watched the news.

When I studied the war in school, I asked
my mother why he didn't go. *He hurt his knee.*
By the time it healed, we had three kids.
I wanted a father who carried a gun,

who wasn't afraid to die. She said, *Even*
if he lived, it would've killed him. He doesn't talk
about the war he didn't fight. *I used to yell*
so much, he says. *I don't know why.* Without

the war, I can't explain his drinking, the rage
he lost as he got older, the awful tenderness
my mother tends. When she serves pork chops,
she cuts meat from bones she buries

in the trash. When my father's called to table,
he pretends not to know what she's done.

My Mother as Florence Nightingale and Bonnie Parker

She didn't really want to save his life,
the scruffy bastard dumb enough to rob
a small-town bank on Saturday morning,
Main Street clogged with trucks, farmers
headed to lunch, the hardware store, the bank
that took in mostly fives and greasy ones—
but he wasn't going to die unless
she grabbed a gun and finished
what he'd started when the only brick
of twenties exploded into orange.

Forced into a ditch, he shot twice, first
breaking out the dye-smeared windshield,
then through and through his shoulder,
missing every bone and most of all his heart.
After the sheriff took his gun they called
my mother in, though they waited a bit,
kicking the dirt while he cried with pain
and frustration. He was bleeding pretty good
but it was the dye that she'd remember,
torn twenties stuck to ankles and arms.

She had to crouch in the back to reach him—
evidence collection, or the driver's door
was too bashed in—and I sometimes slip,
see her as a hostage pinned by fear
and forceful turns. Reluctant at first,
she might lean forward, urge him faster,
find the road to a secret life. And if they chose
to die in a blaze of blacktop glory,
she'd know exactly where to shoot.

Blood Drive

In college I gave blood for homecoming, finals,
Valentine's, finals again. Some nurses said
sweetie and *hon*, patted hands, asked about classes.

The ones I wanted moved from cot to cot:
Uncross your legs. Make a fist and squeeze.
Don't watch the needle. I always did, willing

my blood to leave faster, to fill the bag
in record time. Once, I fainted before I was finished,
once needed an hour to give enough. I kept

going back, practicing for war or natural disaster,
the ambulance my mother drove. Released
to the snack table, cotton ball taped to the wound,

I turned down cookies, stickers, thanks from volunteers,
then—dizzy, weightless—walked to my dorm.
Each time, I told my mother only after. *You'll make*

yourself sick, she warned. Each time the cot,
the needle, what I needed to prove—*see what I can do*
without you, hurt myself for someone else.

False Positive

Tearing pain in the produce section, blood
staining my jeans as I reached for the broccoli.

A checker helped me to my car, laid her apron
on the seat. Traffic lights were red or turning

as I drove. I thought about signs, if I
should pray, be grateful my body decided

without my help. Every nurse who touched me
wore a wedding band. After the exam I waited,

saw blood-brown smears on my fingers, strap
of my purse. The doctor opened the door,

my chart: the cramps and blood belonged
to my period, two months delayed, brain and body

producing symptoms—nausea, weight gain,
shadow of a heartbeat behind my own—I believed

without a test or doctor's visit. How relieved
I should have been. How real my grief.

How to Find Your Missing Child

From guidelines published by the US Department of Justice

Choose pictures that resemble your child. Describe scars, birthmarks, missing teeth. *Put someone persuasive in charge of fliers. People with information may visit liquor and adult video stores more often than banks, post offices, and schools.* Unlike German shepherds, bloodhounds can follow your child's scent even if he or she was in a vehicle or someone's arms. *Don't clean your child's room, empty your trash, touch anything with your child's fingerprints, DNA, or scent: hairbrushes, bedding, dirty clothes.* Media interest may be intense or lukewarm. You may attain celebrity status. You may be filmed while grocery shopping or getting in your car. *Most law enforcement lack experience with missing children. Expect to be questioned before being cleared as a suspect.* Rewards may or may not encourage a safe return. *Any so-called psychic dream may be an actual observation by someone afraid to get involved.* After the first forty-eight hours, plant a tree, release balloons, organize a marathon or rally. Consider buttons, T-shirts, bumper stickers, baseball-type cards—anything to keep the story alive. *Your boss may be understanding at first, then say you must return to work or be replaced.* Young children will want to celebrate birthdays and holidays despite a missing sibling. *Force yourself to eat and sleep. The nightmare will continue until your child is found.*

Kindred Spirit

My father doesn't say *ghost*, though I know
he's haunted. Instead he says, *When they let
Uncle Marion out of that hospital, he didn't
even move the same. He said they tried to take
his stories.* He loves his fifteen uncles fiercely.
Nearly all of them drank, did time in prison
or mental hospitals, died before forty.

When Marion was twenty, a judge offered him
the navy or prison. *He couldn't swim,
so he ran away.* Then, prison or the army.
Marching hurt his feet. The third time,
he picked prison and was out in six months.
I never liked to hear folks call him crazy,
my father says. *He couldn't help how he was.*

What I know about my father tells me why
he loves these men—the troubles they ran from
and to, stories they lived without learning
what they meant—and why he mourns.
Each time my father had a choice, he chose
the world he already knew, holding still
till what he wanted looked like what he had.

Attachment Disorder

> Reborns [are] incredibly lifelike baby dolls that sell for up to $4,000 to adult
> women who collect them, change their clothes, and in some ways treat them
> like real babies.
> —TODAY.COM

As a child, I loved squirrels, feral cats,
abandoned dogs I saw on TV, the family of dolls
I carried everywhere even after my friends
all switched to Barbie, with her boyfriend
and high-heeled shoes. Every few months
my mother asked, *You know your dolls aren't real,*
don't you? and I'd cry when I tried to explain
how much they needed me. I thought by thirty-five
I'd have a husband, babies. People say *adopt*
but they don't know how hard it is, every bit
of your life recorded on triplicate forms,
nowhere to write what they're really asking:
I'm not crazy, abusive, won't leave my baby
home alone while I buy drugs, abandon her
if she has colic, allergies, an ugly nose.
When I saw the website—so many faces
I could choose, fists closed or open, fine hairs
attached by hand—I knew I'd found
a second chance. I didn't mother my dolls
as well as people thought: I played favorites,
screamed and jerked their arms, neglected them
for weeks, then woke them up and changed
their clothes, hurt they hadn't missed me.
My new baby will breathe, feel warm and heavy
when I hold her. She'll be as real as I deserve.

My Mother's Place

I cooked meals—fried meat and gravy, biscuits
popped from a tube—too heavy for the heat,
offered one more beer before I filled Dad's plate.
At the supper table, I sat in my mother's place.

He wished to hell that she'd stay home, save us
instead of strangers. Mornings, my mother's eyes
were swollen, red, quick to see my spills.
You don't really need me here, not the way

my patients do. I put away her cast-iron skillet,
its handle slick with grease, folded a dish towel
I'd let sour. The house was mine till she came home.
Even Dad sometimes forgot, asked for meals

or mending I couldn't fix. *You have to do better
than this.* I sorted silverware into its drawer—
knife, spoon, fork with crusted tines. I couldn't hide
the mess I left, how bad I was at being her.

Mother-Loss

Linda Zapata last saw her mother Jeanette on October 11, 1976. She was
eleven years old.

I thought she left because I wouldn't clean
my plate, room, hamster's cage. Because
I talked back, outgrew my shoes too fast.

Because she was tired, stressed, upset
by the divorce, in love with a man who wanted
to leave Wisconsin and my whiny voice.

Because my father followed her to work
and her boyfriend's apartment, borrowed
my house key to search her closet, dresser,

checkbook. I was thirty before I could say,
My mother disappeared, before I knew
I'd need her all my life. Decades after

her death, police reopened the case. My father
killed her with a paperweight, his choking hands,
hid her body in the crawl space before

I came home from school, then buried her
in a vacant lot. He'll serve three years
for what he calls *an accident*. Sometimes

I hated her for leaving me, for making me afraid
it was my fault. I hope she'll forgive
my anger, years I grieved for me instead of her.

Changeling

At fourteen, I've lost my magic, can't find
my way in the woods, feel weather change
against my skin, strike fire without flint.
My muscles strain against bone, skin chafes

and itches. Words drop from my mouth
like clods of dirt, trip me if I talk too fast.
When I walk, the earth should shake, birds fall
from trees. A hundred years I ran through field

and forest looking for a family where I'd fit,
a boy who knew he didn't belong, whose life
would be easy to steal. I wanted a home
that wasn't a hollow log, cave that smelled of rot.

Seven years I've lived among these people,
each day less able to survive without
fresh water, milk and meat at every meal.
They can't see I'm not their son, have forgotten

how to find proof. If they cooked my dinner
in an eggshell, held me over a fire or made
me laugh, I'd have to tell the truth. If he survives,
the boy whose place I took will learn to love

the woods, the powers I once had. Like me,
he'll learn to live without what came before.

Saint Sister

She smells like lint and peanut butter, chews
her hair into sticky ropes. In the morning,
Mom has to make sure she's really showered,
not just wet her hair, sprayed my perfume.
She gets straight As, says B is for *Busty*,
Bimbo, Bitch. Even with earphones, I can hear
her practice piano, the same song for hours,
days. She almost always wins, the judges,
audience, in love from the first note,
my parents beaming at their genius daughter.
Ever since she disappeared—walking home
from school because I forgot to pick her up—
the girl on the posters, DVD my uncle made,
seems like a stranger, her hair unchewed,
back soldier-straight when she takes the stage.
On the news, I have to say she's my best friend
even though she's only twelve, that I miss her music,
miss eating ice cream while we watch *Oprah*.
My sister bites her nails and spits them
on my bed. She steals from me, borrows jewelry
she breaks or loses, cries because her wrists
and fingers ache, because being perfect
makes her tired. If we don't look for who
she really is, I'm afraid we'll never find her.

Custody Battle

In my yellow dining room, my brother empties
one beer after another, pushing away the sandwich
he needs to eat. A court order keeps him
from drinking near his daughters. *Bullshit,*

he says, gets up for another. When he sits down,
he tells me he's happy I don't remember how
our parents fought: *It was better after you were born.*
The nights Mom worked, I watched Dad drink,

watched for anger or sadness, counted the cans
on the table, in the trash. I say, *Dad knows*
he did things wrong. My brother cries. I reach
across the table, take his hand as I would Dad's.

Our fingers slip, let go. In Omaha, he tries and fails
to get his daughters back. In my fridge, one beer
still hooked in its plastic ring. I wait three days
to taste its bitter foam, my brother's, father's breath.

Home Security

Dead bolts, window locks, alarm, guns
always loaded, within reach. A delivery driver
was pistol-whipped just down the street.
The liquor store was robbed. When I left
for work, she locked the door behind me.
She called when she got in her car, called
again from her job, the store, to tell me
she was safe. At home, we practiced moving
through dark rooms to surprise an intruder,
spoke in code: *I need a drink* meant *Check
the living room. I think I'll watch TV* meant
*Go upstairs, lock yourself in the bathroom,
and call the police.* Saturday night,
shotgun finally fixed and loaded, I walked
to the bedroom to put it away—we hadn't
done our drills. When I swept the kitchen,
she turned from the stove, cocked her thumb
and index finger. My trigger made her chest
explode. Out on bond, I'm not allowed to hunt
or handle guns. I leave the curtains open,
doors unlocked, alarm turned off. Without
my wife, there's nothing to defend.

Wish List

The doctor told me that if she did anything again that she would be able to hear again first. He told me to talk to her. He told me to ask her for small things.
—MICHAEL KIMBALL, *How Much of Us There Was*

Button, paper clip, piece of gum, shortcut
to the freeway. The likelihood of rain. Stamp,
straight pin, coffee to drink on the porch.
After every question I'd wait a minute, sometimes

two, knowing any sound might be an answer,
that she might wake confused. I rubbed lotion
on skin surrounded by tubes, helped nurses change
her sheets, flexed her arms and legs so she'd

be strong when she woke up. I asked for aspirin,
ice cream, where she kept the extra flour, key
to the garage. Sometimes I asked her to open
her eyes, squeeze my hand, but those were cheating

because they weren't small. What time it was,
how much my socks should cost. The doctor
didn't say what to do when she didn't wake up,
when all the ways I needed her weren't enough

to bring her back. *Small things*, he'd said,
but I don't know how her grave can hold them all,
how I can live without cough drops, clean
handkerchiefs, her hand to hold when I'm afraid.

Dispatch

This is not an emergency, I say
when Mom picks up. She answers,
Hold on, we're getting a page.
Two electronic tones, the call numbers
that follow. As a teenager, I listened
to the police scanner in our kitchen,
taught myself the radio codes
that told me where she was, what she
was putting right. Today I wait
without hearing anything I understand.
She's used to waiting—for calls
to come in, units to go out, her shift
to end. She says she doesn't miss
the ambulance, hefting cots and equipment,
the urgent drives. As a dispatcher,
she gets to stay inside, wear
her own clothes, go home unbloodied.
On the night shift, she reads cookbooks
and crime novels next to her keyboard,
wanting and not wanting something
to happen. Mornings at my desk,
I imagine her voice sending sirens
exactly where they're needed.

How It Heals

The technician twists my foot one way,
then the other until I scream. My father
curls his fists. My mother looks at him,

then me, follows him into the hall.
I can see the raw edges of his bones,
breaks he left unset. Three in his nose,

six in his ribs, fingers cracked like glass
he's broken, a dent in his skull shaped
by a mis-swung hammer. I know

he was wild. He must've hurt like hell.
Later, my mother leans into my ear.
Straighten up, she says. *Your dad*

is scared to death. Because we can't
protect his body—fingertips smashed black
and purple, cartilage ground away

from joints, skin torn by wire and steel—
we try to protect him from what hurts us,
even a hairline fracture earned at practice.

He won't let me leave for school until
he tests me on my crutches, arms tight
across his chest. Slowly, I make it

to the kitchen door, then down three steps.
Slowly, I learn what he already knows:
what's broken matters less than how it heals.

Second Act

I know exactly how many hours, days,
engagements we have left, how many boxes
I can fill with suits and campaign shoes,
books about his first term. I miss driving,

being alone, an afternoon to read a book
straight through. He'll be lost without his aides
and advisors, officials who have to take
his calls. I've tried to talk him through

our future, the traveling we could do, hobbies
or projects we might take up, but he ignores
what he can't imagine. He told me long ago
he doesn't believe in polls, approval ratings,

responding to critics, a stance I admired
until I saw its cost—his bewildered mouth
and stubborn chin, shoulders hunched
by his mistakes. They say Lincoln aged

ten years for every one the war was on,
but if he'd survived his second term,
he could've gone back to Springfield,
argued the occasional case—there were places

he was welcome. The offers of seats
on boards, consulting jobs, head of this or that
division have disappeared. I've suggested
a foundation, ways we could give back,

but he'd rather die by assassination, a stroke
in his sleep, than live without the world
watching. At its root, *retirement* means his two
least favorite things—*withdrawal* and *retreat*.

The Woman Who Can't Forget: 25th High School Reunion

Women hug and squeal. Men put arms
around my shoulders, tell me I look good.
They ask me to pose for pictures, settle
disputes—who blew up the science lab,
which year the football team won state.
No one remembers I ate lunch in the library,
got stood up for senior prom. They don't
remember themselves: Susan spread rumors—
who was gay, pregnant, doing drugs—
we couldn't believe or ignore. Andrew
asked me out to win a dare. Laura ran laps
until she fainted, wore sweaters to hide
her starving arms. I was fat, awkward,
so desperate to be liked I couldn't be.
I thought tonight we'd make amends,
admit the misery that turned us against
ourselves, each other. Instead, we pretend
to wish we'd stayed in touch, pretend
to forget what we can't forgive. If I speak up,
they'll remember we weren't friends.
If I don't, I'll never know if I'm the only one
whose true self hasn't changed.

Family Resemblances

My brother's head is in his arms. My father
looks at nothing. At the sink, my mother
washes blood from a C-collar. I pour coffee
into my black cup. She turns off the water,
taps the collar against the sink. *Who died?* I ask.
Unlike my brother, I've lived these mornings
before—when three of my father's friends
rolled their truck on a gravel road,
when the high school burned, when my sister
almost died. I know to move slow and quiet,
check the laundry for blood, clean what I can.

Later, my mother holds my arm too hard:
the phone ringing again and again,
voices saying *crash* and *accident* and finally,
There's a Shipers boy dead in a ditch.
My brother's empty bed. I imagine my father
driving through the dark, my mother rushing
to what hurt, the red-blond hair of a boy
who could've been her son. I imagine
my brother stranded in the crowd, my father
clenching his shoulder, those first angry tears.

Our cousin survived. His girlfriend didn't.
When no one else can hear, my brother says,
I didn't know what could happen, Carrie.
I didn't know. Each time my mother tells
the story, I hear what she won't say:
her fear that a Missouri blacktop would end
the life my brother had made in Arizona,
that his death would kill my father.

Because this is a grief I can't imagine,
I start with what I know: my father
looks away from blood that isn't his.
For another ten years, my brother drinks.
My mother saves more than she can keep.
Because I imagine the stories she won't tell,
I know I'm more like her than I'm like them.

Acknowledgments

Grateful acknowledgment is made to the publications in which some of these poems first appeared (sometimes in slightly different form):

Alaska Quarterly Review: "The Woman Who Can't Forget: Flooding"
Antigonish Review: "Elizabeth King Explains Why *Pupil*, Her One-Half Life-Size Sculpture, Is a Self-Portrait" and "Kill Switch"
Artful Dodge: "Portrait"
Blue Collar Review: "Home Security"
Blue Earth Review: "White Lung"
CALYX Journal: "Custody Battle"
Cimarron Review: "Landing Gear"
Comstock Review: "Olympia"
Crab Orchard Review: "The Dollmaker's Daughter"
cream city review: "The Woman Who Can't Forget: 25th High School Reunion"
descant: "Memoriam: Flight"
ellipsis: "Trust Jesus:"
failbetter.com: "Appetite"
Hanging Loose: "The Worst"
The Ledge Poetry & Fiction Magazine: "Lost, Damaged, Delayed" and "Treatment Plan"
Louisville Review: "Job Description" and "Saint Sister"
MAYDAY Magazine: "Rescue Conditions" and "Safe Return"
Mid-American Review: "Medical History"
minnesota review: "War Stories"
North American Review: "Craftsmanship" and "Renovation"
Pearl: "My Mother's Place"
Poetry East: "Inheritance"
River Styx: "Marriage" and "The Woman Who Can't Forget: Self-Storage"
Roanoke Review: "Shelbina Jailbreak" and "Waiting for Spring"
Southern Humanities Review: "Father and Son," "November, 1964," and "Organ Failure"
Southern Poetry Review: "House Rules" and "Whereabouts, Last Known"
Sou'wester: "How to Find Your Missing Child"
The Sow's Ear Poetry Review: "Witness"
Zócalo Public Square: "Mechanical Failure"

"Medical History" was reprinted in *American Life in Poetry*.

Some poems also appeared in the chapbook *Rescue Conditions* (Slipstream, 2009).

Thank you to my wonderful teachers, Kathy Fagan, Ted Kooser, Hilda Raz, and the late David Citino, who helped me realize I had something to say. Thank you to my husband, Randal Long, and to my best, first reader, Andrea Scarpino. Thank you also to all the friends who believed in and helped improve my poems: Drew Blanchard, Jill Khoury, Bob Loss, Kelly McGuiness, and Betsy Wheeler.

I also want to thank the MFA program at the Ohio State University and the English Department at the University of Nebraska–Lincoln for their support.